The
In-Case-of-Emergency
Workbook

The
In-Case-of-Emergency
Workbook

An Essential Life Organizer for You and Yours

Vicki Hinze

Skyhorse Publishing

Skyhorse Publishing books may be purchased in bulk at special discounts for sales promotion, corporate gifts, fund-raising, or educational purposes. Special editions can also be created to specifications. For details, contact the Special Sales Department, Skyhorse Publishing, 307 West 36th Street, 11th Floor, New York, NY 10018 or info@skyhorsepublishing.com.

Skyhorse® and Skyhorse Publishing® are registered trademarks of Skyhorse Publishing, Inc.®, a Delaware corporation.

Visit our website at www.skyhorsepublishing.com.

10 9 8 7 6 5 4

Library of Congress Cataloging-in-Publication Data is available on file.

Cover design by Jane Sheppard
Cover photo by iStock

Print ISBN: 978-1-5107-1810-4

Printed in China

With gratitude to all the professionals who assist us,
including my own:

Dr. Mark Schroeder
Dr. Christopher Reid
Dr. Samuel Poppell
Lydia Sykes, Bruce, and their assistants
ER pros and first responders

TABLE OF CONTENTS

✳

This document contains private and confidential information.
Should an emergency arise and I am unable to speak or act for myself,
please contact the following person immediately:

MY ICE CONTACT	
NAME	
RELATIONSHIP	
ADDRESS	
PHONE	
CELL PHONE	

AUTHOR'S NOTE

A year ago, I got the flu. I took a fourth of a prescribed medication and went to bed. Nine hours later, I woke up parched, went to the kitchen to get a drink of water, and blacked out. My husband found me unconscious in a pool of blood on the kitchen floor. It took two months to fully recover. Two months during which I realized how little anyone knew about what really goes on around here; where I keep things, who we deal with on household matters, etc. And I asked myself, *if my family floundered this much when they could ask me for answers, just how difficult would it be for them if they couldn't, or if I wasn't in a position to tell them?*

It was difficult on us all, and it could have been worse. It could have been a time of even higher anxiety for them if they were forced to try to figure things out on their own. That's the history behind *The In-Case-of-Emergency Workbook*; to help reduce anxiety—in me, and in them. I thought that if I was in this position, others likely are, too. And so, I decided to make this workbook available for others. This is it—and I hope it serves to ease your mind, and the minds of your loved ones, as much as it has mine.

Please note that I am not an attorney; I'm an author, trying to pass along a tool to spare you the lessons I learned the hard way. Requirements in your state or country could be (and likely are) different, so consult professionals in your area on matters where you are uncertain of exactly what is needed to fulfill your wishes. When completed, this document will contain a lot of private information that is essential. Take precautions to protect it and yourself. In these days of identity theft, it is imperative that you make sure your information is available if needed but only to those you wish to have it, and only when you wish them to have it. If you're uncertain how to best handle that, ask your attorney for advice.

A great deal of what follows is the stuff of routine, everyday life—for you. But others, even loved ones with whom you reside, will not know much of it unless they deal with it on a regular basis. That's why it's essential. May this workbook be helpful and comforting to you and yours—and may you have it and not need it for a very long time!

STRONGLY CONSIDER:
1. Putting this workbook in your safe-deposit box.
2. Filing it with your attorney.
3. Scanning it to a CD that is password protected.
4. Having your Trustee or Executor retain it in a safe place.

IMPORTANT NOTE:
Some entities will require a notarized authorization from you to permit anyone other than you to access your account or to act on your behalf. Some permit you to add an individual for emergency situations and some don't, so check with your entities (business or financial institution) so you know for sure you've complied with their requirements.

Blessings,
Vicki Hinze

PERSONAL INFORMATION

NAME	
BIRTH DATE	
PLACE OF BIRTH CITY, STATE, COUNTRY	
SOCIAL SECURITY NUMBER	
GENDER	
MARITAL STATUS	
MAIDEN NAME (IF ANY)	
MOTHER'S NAME	
FATHER'S NAME	
BIRTH CERTIFICATE WHERE A COPY IS LOCATED	

CHILDREN

NAME AND CONTACT INFORMATION	CONTACT	
	YES	NO

OTHER PERSONAL INFORMATION

Home

ADDRESS

_____

Street   *City*   *State*   *Zip*

☐ I own or co-own this home.   ☐ I rent this home.

CO-OWNER OR LANDLORD	
NAME	
ADDRESS	
PHONE	

MORTGAGE LENDER	
NAME	
ACCOUNT NUMBER	
ADDRESS	
PHONE	
☐ I do not have a mortgage on this home.	

INSURANCE CARRIER

COMPANY AND AGENT	
ACCOUNT NUMBER	
ADDRESS	
PHONE	

PROPERTY TAXES

PAYABLE TO	
ID NUMBER TAX ASSESSOR'S PARCEL NUMBER	
AMOUNT	
PHONE	

☐　　I escrow my taxes with my mortgage lender.

☐　　I pay my property taxes direct to the tax collector.

UTILITIES

FOR	ACCOUNT NUMBER	COMPANY	ADDRESS	PHONE
POWER				
GAS				
WATER				
SEWER				
TRASH				
TELEPHONE				
MOBILE				
CABLE				
INTERNET				
HOME ALARM				

OTHER IMPORTANT INFORMATION ABOUT MY HOME

Examples of other information about the home could include the code to arm or disarm the alarm system, the code word required by a monitoring service, the location of the water shut-off valve or the electricity circuit breaker box, or where one could find a spare house key.

SECONDARY RESIDENCE

☐   I do have a secondary residence.

☐   I do not own or lease a secondary residence.

_____

Street   *City*   *State*   *Zip*

☐ I own or co-own this home.   ☐ I rent or lease this home.

CO-OWNER OR LANDLORD	
NAME	
ADDRESS	
PHONE	

MORTGAGE LENDER	
NAME	
ACCOUNT NUMBER	
ADDRESS	
PHONE	

14

INSURANCE CARRIER

COMPANY AND AGENT **ACCOUNT NUMBER**	
ADDRESS	
PHONE	

PROPERTY TAXES

PAYABLE TO	
ID NUMBER TAX ASSESSOR'S PARCEL NUMBER	
AMOUNT	
☐ **I escrow my taxes with my mortgage lender.**	
☐ **I pay my property taxes direct to the tax collector.**	

UTILITIES

FOR	ACCOUNT NUMBER	COMPANY	ADDRESS	PHONE
POWER				
GAS				
WATER				
SEWER				
TRASH				
TELEPHONE				
MOBILE				
CABLE				
INTERNET				
HOME ALARM				

OTHER IMPORTANT INFORMATION ABOUT MY HOME

Examples of other information about the home could include the code to arm or disarm the alarm system, the code word required by a monitoring service, the location of the water shut-off valve or the electricity circuit breaker box, or where one could find a spare house key.

Other Properties

ADDITIONAL PROPERTIES
I OWN/LEASE

ADDITIONAL PROPERTIES		
PROPERTY LOCATION	PARCEL ID NUMBER	LENDER CONTACT INFORMATION

OTHER PROPERTY INFORMATION

If an additional property is rented, include the renter's name, address, and phone number above. Include rental agreement or lease information and where a copy of the lease is located. If an additional property is mortgaged, include the lender and contact information above. Also include where a copy of the mortgage or deed of trust is located.

Financial

BANKING

Enter the type of account (checking, savings, money market, CD, etc.), and other relevant information.

BANKING				
TYPE	ACCOUNT NUMBER	BANK NAME AND CONTACT	BANK ADDRESS	BANK PHONE

IMPORTANT INFORMATION ABOUT THESE BANK ACCOUNTS	
ACCOUNT NUMBER	WHAT I WANT YOU TO KNOW

DEBIT CARDS		
ACCOUNT NUMBER	BANK	PIN NUMBER

CREDIT CARDS

Enter the account number, type of card (Visa, MasterCard, American Express, etc.), the entity issuing the card (Chase, Citibank, your local bank, etc.), and the three or four digit security code on the back of your card.

CREDIT CARDS			
ACCOUNT NUMBER	TYPE	ISSUED BY	CODE

ADDITIONAL INFORMATION I WANT YOU TO KNOW	
ACCOUNT NUMBER	INFORMATION

INVESTMENTS

INVESTMENTS				
TYPE	ACCOUNT NUMBER	CONTACT	SECURITY	OTHER

BROKER	
ACCOUNT NUMBER	
NAME	
ADDRESS	
EMAIL	
PHONE	

Other Information needed (Example: location of stock certificates, bonds, etc.).

WHAT	WHERE

SAFE-DEPOSIT BOX

NOTE: Authorization to access is routinely required. Check with your institution to make sure you have filed what is needed for your wishes to be in effect.

(Check one)

☐ **I do have a safe-deposit box.**

☐ **I do not have a safe-deposit box.**

SAFE-DEPOSIT BOX		
WHERE	**KEY LOCATION**	**BOX NUMBER AND SECURITY INFORMATION**

WHAT I WANT YOU TO KNOW ABOUT WHAT IS IN THIS BOX

HOME SAFE

(Check one)

☐ I do have a home safe.

☐ I do not have a home safe.

HOME SAFE		
WHERE IS SAFE LOCATED?	**KEY LOCATION**	**COMBINATION**

(Check one)

☐ I do have a safe storage device.

☐ I do not have a safe storage device.

SAFE STORAGE DEVICE	
LOCATION	**ACCESS REQUIREMENTS**

(Check one)

☐ **I do have a secret hiding place.**

☐ **I do not have a secret hiding place.**

SECRET HIDING PLACE(S)	
WHERE IT IS	**WHAT IS IN IT**

Special Instructions regarding my safe-deposit box, its contents, my safe storage device, its contents, and/or my secret hiding place(s) and contents.

☐ **Access only in case of my death.**

☐ **Do not access. My Executor or Trustee will handle this.**

☐ **Access only for the following, specific purpose:** _____

AUTHORITY TO ACCESS ONLY UNDER THE FOLLOWING CONDITIONS AND CIRCUMSTANCES

OTHER PERTINENT FINANCIAL INFORMATION

OTHER PERTINENT FINANCIAL INFORMATION

Medical

ALLERGIES

MEDICINES	FOOD	OTHER

PRIMARY MEDICAL INSURANCE

POLICY NUMBER	
COMPANY	
ADDRESS	
PHONE	

SECONDARY MEDICAL INSURANCE

POLICY NUMBER	
COMPANY	
ADDRESS	
PHONE	

DOCTORS

NAME	PHONE	TREATMENT FOR

KNOWN MEDICAL CONDITIONS

CONDITION	DOCTOR

PHARMACY

NAME	PHONE	PRESCRIPTION NUMBER

PRESCRIPTION MEDICATIONS

DRUG	DOSAGE	FREQUENCY	DOCTOR

OVER-THE-COUNTER MEDICATIONS

DRUG	DOSAGE	FREQUENCY

SURGERIES

DATE	TYPE	DOCTOR

LIVING WILL

(Check one)

☐ I do have a living will.

☐ I do not have a living will.

LIVING WILL LOCATION

DO NOT RESUSCITATE INSTRUCTIONS

(Check one)

☐ I do have a a DNR (do not resuscitate) order.

☐ I do not have a DNR (do not resuscitate) order.

LOCATION OF DO NOT RESUSCITATE ORDER

MEDICAL POWER OF ATTORNEY

(Check one)

☐ I do have a medical power of attorney.

☐ I do not have a medical power of attorney.

LOCATION OF MEDICAL POWER OF ATTORNEY

APPOINTEE'S CONTACT INFORMATION	
NAME	
ADDRESS	
PHONE	
EMAIL	

OTHER IMPORTANT MEDICAL INFORMATION

OTHER IMPORTANT MEDICAL INFORMATION

Legal

ATTORNEY	
NAME	
ADDRESS	
PHONE	
EMAIL	

WILL

(Check one)

☐ **I do have a will.**

☐ **I do not have a will.**

WILL	
EXECUTOR/ TRUSTEE NAME	
ADDRESS	
PHONE	
LOCATION OF WILL	

IMPORTANT LEGAL DOCUMENTS

TYPE OF DOCUMENT	REGARDING	DOCUMENT LOCATION

TAX PREPARATION AND RECORDS

(Check one)

☐ I am exempt from paying federal and state income taxes.

☐ I am not exempt from paying federal and state income taxes.

(Check one)

☐ I do prepare my own federal and state income taxes.

☐ I do not prepare my own federal and state income taxes.

TAX PREPARER OR CPA (CERTIFIED PUBLIC ACCOUNTANT)	
NAME	
FIRM	
ADDRESS	
PHONE	

(Check one)

☐ I file federal taxes under my social security number.

☐ I file federal taxes under a Federal Tax Identification Number.

SOCIAL SECURITY NUMBER OR FEDERAL TAX IDENTIFICATION NUMBER

LOCATION OF TAX RECORDS

STATE INCOME TAXES

(Check one)

☐ I do have to pay state income tax.

☐ I do not have to pay state income tax.

STATE INCOME TAXES	
STATE	**CONTACT INFORMATION**
LOCATION OF STATE TAX RECORDS	

OTHER TAXES I PAY			
TYPE	**PAY TO**	**CONTACT INFORMATION**	**FOR**

FINAL ARRANGEMENTS

(Check one)

☐ I have preplanned my final arrangements.

☐ I have not preplanned my final arrangements.

PREPLANNED FINAL ARRANGEMENTS DOCUMENTS LOCATION

FINAL ARRANGEMENT PREFERENCES

(Check one) ☐ BURIAL ☐ CREMATION		
WHERE		
TYPE OF SERVICE		
CLERGY		

SPECIFIC PREFERENCES

OTHER LEGAL INFORMATION

Auto

(Check one)

☐ I do drive.

☐ I do not drive.

DRIVER'S LICENSE		
STATE	LICENSE NUMBER	LICENSE LOCATION

(Check one)   (Check one)

☐ I do own a vehicle.   ☐ I do lease a vehicle.

☐ I do not own a vehicle.   ☐ I do not lease a vehicle.

VEHICLES I OWN/LEASE		
VIN NUMBER	MAKE/MODEL	YEAR

(Check one)

☐ **I do have a loan or lease on my vehicle.**

☐ **I do not have a loan or lease on my vehicle.**

VEHICLE LOAN OR LEASEHOLDER	
NAME	
ADDRESS	
PHONE	
ACCOUNT NUMBER	

VEHICLE INSURER	
AGENT	
COMPANY	
ADDRESS	
PHONE	
POLICY NUMBER	

VEHICLE TITLE

STATE ISSUED TITLE	
TITLE NUMBER	
LOCATION OF TITLE	
OTHER	

LOCATION OF KEYS AND VEHICLE

LOCATION OF VEHICLE KEYS	
LOCATION OF VEHICLE	
OTHER	

OTHER VEHICLE INFORMATION

Personal Property

PERSONAL PROPERTY		
ITEM	LOCATION OF ITEM	DISPOSITION OF ITEM

PERSONAL PROPERTY

ITEM	LOCATION OF ITEM	DISPOSITION OF ITEM

PERSONAL PROPERTY

ITEM	LOCATION OF ITEM	DISPOSITION OF ITEM

PERSONAL PROPERTY		
ITEM	LOCATION OF ITEM	DISPOSITION OF ITEM

PERSONAL PROPERTY

ITEM	LOCATION OF ITEM	DISPOSITION OF ITEM

PERSONAL PROPERTY		
ITEM	LOCATION OF ITEM	DISPOSITION OF ITEM

Passwords

DEVICES

DEVICE/ LOCATION	SERIAL NUMBER	USER ID	PASSWORD

DEVICES

DEVICE/ LOCATION	SERIAL NUMBER	USER ID	PASSWORD

ONLINE ACCOUNTS

ACCOUNT	URL	USER NAME	PASSWORD

ONLINE ACCOUNTS

ACCOUNT	URL	USER NAME	PASSWORD

Personal Requests

PERSONAL REQUESTS

PERSONAL REQUESTS

BONUS

When emergency responders are called to your home and you're unable to speak for yourself, they look to obvious places for ICE information. Help them help you and put your ICE contact where they can find it. Tear out the ICE contact cards on the following page for your refrigerator, vehicle glove box, and/or your wallet.

IN-CASE-OF-EMERGENCY CONTACT
NAME _____
ADDRESS _____
PHONE _____
NEIGHBOR _____

IN-CASE-OF-EMERGENCY CONTACT
NAME _____
ADDRESS _____
PHONE _____
NEIGHBOR _____

IN-CASE-OF-EMERGENCY CONTACT
NAME _____
ADDRESS _____
PHONE _____
NEIGHBOR _____

IN-CASE-OF-EMERGENCY CONTACT
NAME _____
ADDRESS _____
PHONE _____
NEIGHBOR _____

IN-CASE-OF-EMERGENCY CONTACT
NAME _____
ADDRESS _____
PHONE _____
NEIGHBOR _____

IN-CASE-OF-EMERGENCY CONTACT
NAME _____
ADDRESS _____
PHONE _____
NEIGHBOR _____

IN-CASE-OF-EMERGENCY CONTACT
NAME _____
ADDRESS _____
PHONE _____
NEIGHBOR _____

IN-CASE-OF-EMERGENCY CONTACT
NAME _____
ADDRESS _____
PHONE _____
NEIGHBOR _____

IN-CASE-OF-EMERGENCY CONTACT
NAME _____
ADDRESS _____
PHONE _____
NEIGHBOR _____

IN-CASE-OF-EMERGENCY CONTACT
NAME _____
ADDRESS _____
PHONE _____
NEIGHBOR _____